On Spider's Point

by
Anna Imgrund

GLOBE FEARON
Pearson Learning Group

Project Editor: Brian Hawkes
Editorial Assistants: Jennifer Keezer, Jenna Thorsland
Editorial Development: ELHI Publishers, LLC
Art Supervision: Sharon Ferguson
Production Editor: Regina McAloney
Electronic Page Production: Debbie Childers
Manufacturing Supervisor: Mark Cirillo
Cover Design: Sharon Ferguson
Illustrator: Steven Cavallo

ISBN 0-130-23294-7
Printed in the United States of America

6 7 8 9 10   07 06 05 04

Globe
Fearon

Pearson Learning Group

1-800-321-3106
www.pearsonlearning.com

Contents

1. So Much for Sea Legs

"You OK, kid?" asks Mack, one of the workers on the boat. "You're looking a little green."

Tyrone holds on to the side of the boat. He has his head over the water, but he is trying hard not to get seasick again.

"Don't you be scared, kid," laughs Mack. "You will be getting your sea legs in no time!"

Tyrone raises his head a little to look at Mack. *I'm not going to get sea legs*, he thinks. *I'm going to die.* "How—much—longer?" Tyrone gets out. His face really does look green in the light of day, and it's all he can do to wait for the man's answer without throwing up on the boat.

"Spider's Point is a ways out here, all right," Mack answers, "but I don't guess it's too far off now." He studies Tyrone a while. "I take it you're here for some time, Ty, seeing as how you have so many bags and all."

"My name is Tyrone," he says. "And what do you care?"

"Just thinking you will need a friend, that's all," says the old seaman. "Things are different where you come from, not at all like Spider's Point. There are people like Red Overlook and his group here — people you want to keep away from. But if you need a friend," Mack goes on, "you just look up Tom Champion. He's a good guy."

"I don't need any friends," says Tyrone as he tries to sit down. "I just need to get off this moving water box!"

"Now, now," laughs Mack. "The *Sea Spider* is a good old girl. You just got to get used to walking on her, kid. With wave after wave after wave coming at you, it can be hard!"

Wave after wave after wave — Oh, no! Tyrone gets up as fast as he can and races back to the side of the boat. *So much for dinner,* he thinks. Mack is finding something to laugh about in all of this.

That, if he were not so sick, would make Tyrone mad enough to fight. But as sick as he is, he sees something that makes him feel a little better.

"A beach!" Tyrone calls out. "Is it Spider's Point?"

"One and the same," says Mack. "We will be putting in right there," he points. "Your bags are down in the hold. Just call if you want some help."

Mack heads off to work on the boat, leaving Tyrone and his green face looking down into the waves of the sea.

What am I doing here? he thinks. *I don't want to live with a grandmother I can't even remember. I really don't like this boat. And Spider's Point is nothing but a little hole-in-the-wall place on a map!* Tyrone gets mad just thinking about the problems that made him come here. Looking back, they don't seem bad enough to make him have to leave home for a year.

As Tyrone looks into the water, a school of fish goes by. *Take me!* he thinks. *Take me anywhere but to Spider's Point and Grandma Inez.* But, as he looks up, the boat is pulling into the Point. D-Day. Time to get off.

"Here you go, Ty," says Mack as he and another guy walk up with some of Tyrone's bags from the hold.

"I said, my name is **Tyrone**!"

"Whatever, kid," says Mack. "But you're on Spider's Point now, and you may as well get used to the way things are out here, right?" With that, Mack hits Tyrone on the back with one of his big hands, and says, "What do you say we get off this boat and get something to eat, everybody?"

Something to eat? That's all it takes for Tyrone to make a mad race back to the side of the boat. *I can't take this place!* he thinks, throwing up whatever insides are still there.

2. The *Venus Light*

"Now, you just sit down here, Ty, and I'll get you something cold to drink," says Grandma Inez. "Those boats can really turn you inside out when you aren't used to them."

"My name is **Tyrone**, and I'm OK."

"Well, **you** can call **me** Gran," she tells him with a smile, "and, if you don't mind my saying so, your face still looks pretty green for someone who's just 'OK.'" Without another word, she goes into the kitchen and comes back with 2 cold drinks. "Try this," she says, sitting down next to him.

Tyrone looks at this woman who is his grandmother. "You know, I really didn't want to come here," he says, thinking he sounds like a monster, but too mad to care.

"And I hope it makes you feel better to say it." Gran smiles. "But you **are** here, and that makes it different." Gran gets up and goes to the window. "The time will fly by! You will see. It's just that— well, right now your mom and dad have some things to work out."

"What you **mean** is that they want me out of the picture," says Tyrone. "I was in the way." The memory is hard. Tyrone finds that, for the first time in a long time, he feels like crying.

"No, no, you're wrong about that," says Grandma Inez. "But they **do** need some time together. And, in the meantime, I'm really happy to have you here with me on Spider's Point. It will be good for all of us."

Good for you, maybe, Tyrone thinks. *Me, I'm out of here.* He gets up and walks over to the fireplace to look at the pictures on the wall.

"That's your dad," says Gran, pointing to one of the pictures, "when he was a little boy."

"You're kidding," says Tyrone. It's hard to believe his dad was ever a kid. But there he is, down at the beach, with a big smile on his face.

"Not at all," says Gran. "He was on his boat, the *Venus Light,* in that picture right after he won a big race."

"Dad raced boats when he was a kid?" Tyrone can't picture it.

"All the time," Gran says with a smile. "Of course, he gave it up when he moved away."

"Did boats make him sick too?" asks Tyrone.

"Oh, no," laughs Gran. "He was used to being on a boat, Ty. It was all I could do to get him to come in for dinner! He wanted to be out on the water from sunup to sundown!"

"Forget that!" says Tyrone. "I like my dinner **in** me, where it belongs." Gran just laughs at that. He turns to her. "Where is the boat now?" Tyrone wants to know.

"The *Venus Light?* Still out back, under the beach house, believe it or not," says Gran, " —just waiting for a boy like you to clean her up and get her going again."

Tyrone gives his grandmother a long look. "You would let me do that?" he asks at last. "That is — if I wanted to?"

"Well, I would have to get someone to show you how, of course," she answers, "but that's no problem."

Tyrone just can't believe it. She would let him use the *Venus Light!* If she's right about boats not **always** making you sick, then maybe his time on Spider's Point won't be so bad after all! But then again, it's been a long time and maybe that boat is just a lot of old wood now. "When can I see it?" he asks.

"Just as fast as your legs will take you, Ty," laughs Gran. "Go outside, turn to the beach and look under the seaside end of the house. She's been waiting for you."

Gran smiles after Tyrone as he races out of the house. *He's had so many problems at home*, she thinks. *Being at Spider's Point is just the thing to put some life and hope back into that boy!* She walks out behind him to see his face as he finds the *Venus Light*. Tyrone's eyes turn into big circles.

Yes, Ty, she says to herself with a smile, *the sea is calling your name even now.*

3. Carmen

"What are you doing?" asks the girl.

"What does it look like I'm doing?" asks Tyrone.

"It looks like you're trying to fight a wooden monster," laughs the girl.

Tyrone stops cleaning up the boat and turns to look at her. "Don't you have anything better to do?" he asks.

"No. Can't think of a thing." She walks closer to see what he's up to.

"You the one who was throwing up all over the *Sea Spider* last week?" she asks.

Tyrone's face turns red, but he doesn't say a word.

"You know, Mack said it was a boy who looked just like you," she says. "It **was** you throwing up on the *Sea Spider*, right?"

"Look, you're really getting in my way here, whoever you are," says Tyrone, turning green. "Why don't you go — go — **fish** or something?"

"That's what I guessed," says the girl, smiling. "It **was** you! Mack said it was something to see! Said you were as green as money then too," she laughs. "In fact — "

"OK, it **was** me!" says Tyrone. "Why don't we let the TV people know? Maybe get it out from one end of the U.S. to the other? **Spider's Point Kid Throws Up?** In big letters over the TV? Would that make you happy?"

"Guess you're still feeling sick, aren't you?" says the girl.

"No, I'm not sick!" Tyrone says, getting mad again. "Just sick of you!" And, mad as can be, he gets down from the boat, takes hold of the side, and pulls it far down the beach, away from the girl.

He hopes she will leave.

She doesn't.

Walking up to him again, with a look of know-how on her face, the girl says, "You know, that part doesn't go there — not if you want to take the boat out to sea, anyway."

14

"And how would you know?" Tyrone asks, putting the part down as if that had been his idea all along.

"I have lived on Spider's Point all my life," she says. "Spider's Point people know all there is to know about boats."

"Well, I don't need any help," says Tyrone. "I know something about boats myself."

Why did I say that? I know nothing about boats! Tyrone thinks.

Why did he say that? He knows nothing about boats! the girl thinks. "Then you must know that you're putting that part in upside down," she says.

OK, that's it, Tyrone thinks. He takes the part, throws it down on the beach, and walks over to the girl. "Get out of here!" he screams. "I didn't ask you to come here, I don't want you here, and I **don't** like you!"

The girl laughs. "You don't even know me!" she says. "Most people get to know me a little before they don't like me."

"You are — you are — I can't even talk to you!" says Tyrone, going back to the *Venus Light.* "You are out of your mind!"

"But I **do** know how to work with boats," says the girl, a smile in her eyes. "It looks like that's more than you can say. And, just so you know," she says as she runs to keep up with him, "I can put them out on the water, too — without throwing up."

Tyrone is just about to take this kid on, girl or no girl, when Grandma Inez calls down from the beach house. "Oh, Ty! I see you got to meet Carmen!"

Tyrone stops, not knowing what Grandma could be talking about as she makes her way down the beach to them. "I'm so happy you could come over so fast, Carmen," says Gran when she gets to the 2 of them.

"No problem," says Carmen, still smiling.

"Ty, I told you I would get you some help in working on the *Venus Light*," says Grandma Inez, "and here she is!"

"Soooo happy to meet you, Ty," says Carmen as she sticks out her hand.

Oh, no! thinks Tyrone. *And I was thinking the* Sea Spider *was bad!*

4. More Than One Champion

"Gran, where can I get new paint for the *Venus Light*?" asks Tyrone.

"What a good idea!" says Gran. "Here is what you do, Ty," she says. "Just go down Sunquest Drive and keep looking to your right. You will go by a lot of little shops, then an animal shelter. The Paint Shop is there at the end of Sunquest Drive," she tells him, "after the shelter."

"I think I can find it," says Tyrone, getting up to leave.

"Is Carmen going with you?" asks Gran.

Not in this lifetime, thinks Tyrone.

"Not this time," he says.

Before Gran can ask him more about Carmen, Tyrone heads off to find the Paint Shop. *That's all I need*, he thinks. *Some know-it-all girl getting in my way.*

So Tyrone walks down Sunquest Drive alone, happy to be out on a pretty day like this. He passes the shops, looks to his right, and sees the shelter Gran was telling him about. **Tom Champion, DVM**, a sign out front reads.

Tom Champion, Tyrone says to himself. *Isn't that the name of the guy Mack was telling me about on the boat?* He walks over to the shelter and looks in the window. A man waves goodbye to a woman inside and, as she walks out, the man sees Tyrone.

"Well, how do you do?" says the man. "You new in Spider's Point?"

"I'm — uh — I guess so," says Tyrone.

"I'm Tom Champion," says the man, putting out his hand. "What can I do for you?" He waits with a smile.

"I'm Tyrone. When I came over on the *Sea Spider*, Mack said to look you up. I'm here with my grandmother, Inez Card, and I saw your name on the shelter when I was walking by."

"Then you're —"

"Yes, he's the one," comes a sound from behind him. It's that Carmen girl!

She comes into the shelter and walks in back of Tom Champion. She has a hot dog in her hand.

"What are **you** doing here?" asks Tyrone.

"I live here," says Carmen. "This is my dad." She puts the last of the hot dog into her mouth. "What about you? Still trying to get that boat cleaned up on your own?"

Carmen Champion. I just knew it! thinks Tyrone. *This girl is like an insect that will not go away!*

"The *Venus Light* and I are doing OK, just fine," he says.

"Is that right?" she comes back. "I don't know about **you** — let's just say the votes are not in on that one — but the *Venus Light* needs a lot of work."

Tyrone turns to Tom Champion. "Well, nice to meet **you**, anyhow," he says, then waves as he heads off to the Paint Shop.

"Oh, come on," says Carmen, coming after Tyrone, "lighten up! What's your problem with me, anyway?" she wants to know. "Is it because I'm a girl?"

"No," says Tyrone, who keeps walking. "It's because you're — you're — well, **you**!"

He walks on.

She keeps up.

"So, where are you going?" she asks.

"To the Paint Shop," he answers. "And where are you going?" he asks, to make a point.

"With you, of course," she comes back. "You **and** your boat need some big-time help. But I'll start with the boat. It doesn't talk back!"

5. Let's Be Friends

Carmen laughs as she sees Tyrone try to get all three big paint cans down Sunquest Drive and back to the *Venus Light*. He makes it to the animal shelter, then stops and looks at Carmen.

"If you're going to go everywhere I go anyway, then do you mind helping out?" he asks at last.

"Who, me?" she says, as if she can't believe he needs help.

"Yes, you!" he says. "You think these are **light** or something?"

Laughing, she takes a big can from Tyrone, and they start walking again. "Happy now?" she asks. "All you had to do was ask."

Ty looks at her and, at last, gives her a little smile. "I guess so," he answers. Then, "What does your dad do at the shelter?" he wants to know.

"My dad is really into animals," laughs Carmen. "At the shelter, he takes care of sick dogs and cats. On the *Sea Dog*, he studies sharks."

"The *Sea Dog*?" asks Tyrone.

"Our boat," says Carmen. "Dad uses it to study all kinds of sea life, but he's really interested in sharks. To get it all in, he works 1/2 of the time at the shelter, the other 1/2 on the *Sea Dog*."

"Sharks!" says Tyrone. "Is he out of his mind?"

"Of course not," says Carmen. "It's a science. He studies everything about them — where they live, how they live, what they eat — "

"I don't even want to think about what they eat!" says Tyrone.

"Oh, come on. It's interesting," Carmen says.

"Not if it eats me!" Ty comes back.

"Get this," says Carmen. "Did you know that sharks grow new teeth every time the old ones fall out? If you look in a shark's mouth, you will see lots and lots of teeth!" she tells him.

"That's a pretty picture," answers Tyrone. He can't get over thinking about what sharks eat with all those teeth.

Carmen smiles. "If you can ever get over this idea that every shark wants to eat you," she says, "then you will see why my dad studies them."

"If it's all the same to you," laughs Tyrone, "I'll just leave that to you, your dad, and your little friends in the sea."

By this time, they have made it to Gran's house. Carmen and Tyrone put the three paint cans out front, and then Tyrone sticks his head inside the door. "Gran, I'm back."

Grandma Inez comes out of her bedroom with a green plant in one hand and a book in the other. "It's you 2!" she says. "I was just going out in the sun to read a little. Ty, there is some dinner in the kitchen for you when you want it. Enough for you, too, Carmen," Gran calls as she heads out. "Help yourself!"

They go in the kitchen, where Gran has put out a mouthwatering dinner. "Mmmm," says Carmen. "Lots better than a hot dog! Let's eat!" In no time, they have laughed and talked their way through everything Gran cooked. After cleaning up, they get their paint from the front of the house and go down to the beach to work on the *Venus Light*. "I'd like to get started painting before the sun goes down," Tyrone says.

"Don't go so fast!" says Carmen. "Let's do it one time, and do it right, OK?"

As Carmen talks on, she sees that Ty is not hearing her anymore.

"Carmen to Tyrone," she laughs, "come in, Tyrone!"

But his eyes are on the beach. She looks where he is looking, and sees something that is flying end-over-end down the beach. "What is that?" he says, pointing.

"I'll go and see," says Carmen. She runs ahead to get it as Ty puts the paint cans by the boat.

She is taking a closer look at their find as Tyrone walks up. "What did it turn out to be?" he asks.

"I don't know," says Carmen, "but it looks to me like a map!"

6. The Map

"What does it say?" Tyrone wants to know.

"There aren't any words, really," says Carmen. "Just headings, like you would give to someone driving a boat."

"Headings to take you where?" he asks.

"It's hard to tell," says Carmen, "but there is a big X here, and right by it is a picture of something that looks like **money**!"

"Let me see," says Tyrone. She hands it to him, and he studies it for a long time. "Wait. It **does** say something," he tells her.

"What? Where?"

"Down here," Ty says. "It's like someone was writing it down, then changed his mind. But it looks like it reads R-E-D."

"Red?" Carmen says. "I don't get it. Do you?" she asks.

"No," says Tyrone, "but you're right about one thing, Carmen. No question. This is a map to a **lot** of money somewhere out there." He looks out over the sea. "And you know what else?" he asks, looking up at Carmen.

"No, what?" she wants to know.

"Something about this map tells me that this is not on the up-and-up, if you know what I mean," says Tyrone. "I'd better take it to Gran."

"No!" says Carmen. "Don't do that!"

"Why not?" asks Ty.

"Because," she answers, "if it's **not** on the up-and-up, then whoever lost this map is going to come looking for it! They may not be so happy with whoever finds it!"

"Us?" Tyrone says, feeling small.

"Us!" says Carmen, feeling the same way. "And if your Grandma Inez knows about it, then she may not be safe."

"Man," says Tyrone as he hands the map back to her, "why did we ever have to find this in the first place?"

"Now, wait," says Carmen. "Don't get worked up. It may turn out to be harmless."

"So what do we do?" says Ty.

"Well," Carmen says, talking as she thinks it through, "how about this? Let's hide the map for now. Don't tell anyone that we have it. Not a word, OK?"

"Then what?" says Tyrone.

"We will just keep working on the *Venus Light*. After she's painted, and after we have taken her out to see how she does on the sea," says Carmen, "then we can use these map headings to find the money!"

"Good idea!" says Tyrone. "Maybe the money will tell us something about who lost the map. Then, if they're good people, we will give the money back. If not — "

"If not," Carmen says with a dark look, "then we may have some real problems on our hands."

7. Shark Food? No Thanks!

"If you're trying to scare me, Carmen," says Tyrone, "then it's working!"

"Better **scared** than **shark food**," says Carmen. "We are not talking about a kid's bank, here, Tyrone! That looks like a lot of money!"

"Give me the map!" orders Tyrone.

"What are you going to do with it?" Carmen wants to know.

"We will just leave it here on the beach," he says. "That's what we will do — leave it like we never even saw it."

"That works," says Carmen. "But only if the people who lost it don't know that we have seen it."

Tyrone looks all over the beach, and along the houses, feeling open to attack. There are so many places someone could hide. "So what's your idea?" he says at last.

"I vote," says Carmen, "that we hold on to the map. It may be the only thing that saves us. They may need it to get to the money."

Knowing that she is right, Tyrone starts thinking of places to hide the map. "How about hiding it inside the *Venus Light?*" he says. "That keeps it away from Gran, but close to us while we work on the boat."

"That's a good idea!" says Carmen.

They put the map in a safe place on the boat, and then they get back to work.

"We have to look like nothing is wrong," says Tyrone, "in case anyone is keeping an eye on us." They get the paint cans out and start to work on the body of the *Venus Light.*

"You know," says Carmen, hitting an ant off her leg as she paints, "this really is going to look good when we get through. Why did your dad ever leave it?"

"I don't know," says Ty. "I never even knew he raced a boat, or even **had** one."

"Didn't you ever see it when you came to your grandma's?" she asks.

"We never came," says Ty. "We live in the mountains, and never came to Spider's Point."

"So why did you come now?" asks Carmen. "If you don't mind me asking, that is."

"It's OK. My mom and dad weren't doing so well," says Tyrone. "My dad—well, he used to drink, and he just lost his job. I think my mom's scared he'll start drinking again."

"Maybe that's why he went away from Spider's Point in the first place," says Carmen.

"Maybe so," says Tyrone. "I just know that he didn't ever talk about this place, or the people, or what he did as a kid."

"Maybe it was too hard for him."

Tyrone looks at Carmen. "You may be right," he says. "I didn't think about that." He goes back to painting, then looks up again. "How did you get to know so much, Carmen?"

"That's not hard," she says. "It's because I always ask questions, and I never, **never** give up."

"I didn't think you ever, ever stopped talking."

"That too," she says, looking up with a smile.

8. Big Red

"It's taken a while, but we are through at last," the kids say to Grandma Inez.

"Oh, I can't wait to see," Gran says. "Let me get my glasses."

The three of them walk down the beach to the like-new *Venus Light.*

"I just can't believe it," cries Gran as she walks around the boat. "You know, Ty, I don't think she was this pretty even when your dad was here! Just look at all you 2 have done!"

Carmen and Tyrone can't help but smile at the good things Grandma Inez is saying about them. *It* **was** *hard work,* they think. *And it shows! The* Venus Light *looks like she's going out for her first race ever!*

"Can we take her out now, Gran?" asks Tyrone. "I can't wait to try her out!"

"I know, Ty," says Gran, "but you don't know how. That takes some time."

"I'll show him how!" says Carmen.

"I know you would like to," Gran smiles, "but you're going to have to ask your dad first. If it's OK with Tom Champion, then it's OK by me!"

"All right!" scream the 2. "We will be back in no time, Gran," Tyrone calls as they head off to the shelter.

He and Carmen run down Sunquest Drive, and get to the first shops before they have to stop. "Wait, Tyrone," calls Carmen. "That's a long run!"

Ty stops and waits for Carmen. As he waits, however, he hears 2 men in a fight over by the Fish and Game Shop. Tyrone can't help but hear what they are saying.

"You did what?" says the one. "Of all the —"

"Now, it was not all my doing, Red Overlook!" says the other man. "If you remember, it was **your** idea to come up the beach way."

"What are you looking at, kid?"

"But it was **not** my idea to let some kids get hold of—of—" the first man stops and looks up, seeing Tyrone for the first time. "What are you looking at, kid?" he asks. He turns dark eyes to Carmen, too, as she runs up to Ty.

"N-N-Nothing, man," says Tyrone, "not a thing. We were just passing by. We will be on our way." He takes hold of Carmen's hand with a fast, "Come on!"

"Aaaah you! Wait!" screams Red Overlook. "What are your names, you little—" But Carmen and Tyrone are long gone. Ty pulls her all the way to the animal shelter, then into the front door and down a hall. He leaves her to run back to a window, and looks to see if the 2 men are coming after them. *So far, so good,* he thinks. He goes back to Carmen.

"Are they gone?" asks Carmen when she can get the words out.

"I think so," says Tyrone.

"What was that all about?" Carmen wants to know. "Why did we run?"

"Some things made me think we needed to get out of there," says Tyrone. "And fast!"

"And they were?" asks Carmen.

"First, I think 'Overlook' was the last name of the guy Mack told me to keep away from when I came over on the *Sea Spider*.

"And?" says Carmen, thinking that Ty has scared her for nothing.

"**And** the 2 guys were fighting about something they had let some kids get hold of!" says Ty, mad that she doesn't see what he's trying to say.

"But that doesn't mean—" Carmen starts to say.

"**And**, Carmen Champion," Tyrone keeps going, "one man called the other one by the name of 'Red' — Red Overlook! Now do you see?" he says.

Carmen's face looks scared as she thinks of the one small word written on the side of the map: R-E-D.

9. So Far, So Good

"Well, it's you guys," Tom Champion calls out as he sees Tyrone and Carmen in the hall of the shelter. "I was thinking you would be out working on the boat on a day like this!"

"We would be," says Carmen, giving Tyrone a look that says let **me** take care of this, "but we don't need to."

"Is that right?" says her dad. "Why?"

"Our work on the *Venus Light* is over, Dad," says Carmen. "She's clean, she's painted, and she looks like new!"

"Good job!" says Tom Champion as he sets down a chart by his PC. "I can't wait to see it."

"Not right now, Dad," says Carmen. "No time. We really want to take her out and see what she's made of."

Carmen's dad looks up at them. "Then why are you here?"

"Tyrone is new to Spider's Point," Carmen tells him, "and I'm the only one of the 2 of us who knows how to put out the *Venus Light*. Do you care?"

"Yes, I **care**," says her dad, "but no, I don't mind. If you want to, however, you 2 can go out with me on the *Sea Dog* after I'm through here. We can use the cage and show Tyrone some of the sharks I have been studying."

"Sounds like something I'll have to pass up," says Tyrone. "I don't even like using my name in the same sentence as sharks. I really don't want to see them up close, cage or no cage!"

"All right, all right," laughs Tom Champion. "You 2 go on and have a good time, but do be careful out there. Don't go out too far or too long. The *Venus Light* is not the *Sea Dog*. OK?"

"No problem," they say as Carmen's dad goes into another room to look at a sick animal. "See you tonight, Dad," Carmen calls out.

When Carmen's dad closes the door, Tyrone goes over to the front window to look out again. *Good. The men are gone.* "Come on," he calls to Carmen, and one at a time, they go out of the door of the shelter and head to Sunquest Drive. When they get to Sunquest, however, it's like a race as they fly to the beach house as fast as their legs will take them!

"Safe," Carmen calls out as she races through the door.

"Yes, safe," says Tyrone, right behind her. "So far, anyway."

10. The Red Fishing Boat

"Tyrone, you get on that side," says Carmen, "I'll get on this side, and together we will get the boat into the water. 1–2–3, **Go!**"

They run with racing legs, hands on the sides of the boat, as the *Venus Light* goes from beach to water in one liquid move. Behind them, Grandma Inez lets them know how happy she is to see it back on the water again. "This makes me think of so many memories, Tyrone," she calls, trying not to cry. "Your dad will be so happy to know you have given the *Venus Light* new life."

"Can we take her out now, Gran?" asks Tyrone.

"Try and stop her!" she laughs. "Go! Go! And have a good time! Let Carmen show you everything she knows about this old sea!" Then Grandma Inez turns on the beach and walks back to the house, with a stop every now and then to look back at the kids.

Carmen gets them going. Wave falls over wave and smashes into the boat.

"Is everything OK?" asks Tyrone, a little scared of all the waves.

"It's fine!" laughs Carmen. "She moves through the water like a fish!"

For a while, Ty turns light green again. Before too long, however, with Carmen's help, he starts to get used to the up-and-down of the sea. "It's not so bad after all!" he tells Carmen.

"Good. Now, get out the map," orders Carmen. "Take a look at it and tell me where to go from the lighthouse."

"Got it!" says Tyrone as he pulls it out of its hiding place. He studies it, looking at every detail, then points and tells Carmen, "You need to go that way."

"That's a NNE heading, then," says Carmen. They race over the water as far as the map says to go, and then Ty says to turn again. They do everything just as the map describes it, going from point A to point B to point C and so on.

"Where do you think the map is taking us, with all these turns?" asks Tyrone.

"It looks like we are heading to that beach over there," she points. Together, they take the *Venus Light* to a part of the long beach that looks dark. "Well, here we are," says Carmen. "What now?"

Tyrone gets out of the boat and walks around the beach. He studies the map, then walks some more. "It's hard to tell," he says, "but I think the X puts the money somewhere over in here." Carmen walks behind him, looking around.

"Are you scared?" she wants to know.

"Not so far," says Ty. "You?"

"I feel like an insect someone is going to smash!" she says, trying to laugh. "Let's move fast on this and get out of here, OK?"

They keep looking around, but they do not see a place where someone could hide money. Then, out of nowhere, it comes to Tyrone. "It's right here in front of our eyes!" he screams, taking Carmen's hand.

"Not in front of mine, I guess," she says. "I don't see it."

"What was the one word on the map?" asks Tyrone.

'Red,' says Carmen. "It said 'Red'."

"And look over there," points Tyrone.

Carmen just about screams as her eyes fall upon a big red wooden fishing boat turned upside down on the beach.

"**Now** I'm scared," says Tyrone.

They walk over to the fishing boat and circle around it, scared to turn it over and just as scared **not** to.

"Well, we had better take a look," says Tyrone. "It's big, isn't it?"

"We can do it," says Carmen. "Let's try what we did with the *Venus Light* today, but this time we will work from the same side!"

"That sounds good to me," Tyrone says.

"This is it," says Carmen. "1–2–3, **go!**"

Pulling up together, they raise the red fishing boat up and over.

At first they don't say a thing. Then, at last, Tyrone gets his words out: "We have a problem."

"We have a problem."

For there, under the red boat, is a big box packed with more bags of money than Tyrone has ever seen! And on the side of the box are the words "First National Bank of Spider's Point."

These are not good people.

This is not good news.

11. Nobody Home

"What are we going to do with all this money?" Carmen asks.

"Nothing," says Tyrone.

"Nothing?" she comes back. "We are just going to leave it here?"

"We have to," says Ty. "If those men find out we have been here, they will take off with the money before we can tell the cops that it's here — if they can find their way to it, anyhow."

"That, or they could even come after us," says Carmen.

"That's right," Ty tells her. "So we have to leave it here, and come back with the Spider's Point cops."

"And we have to tell my dad and your grandmother," says Carmen. "Right away! They really need to know. Those men could harm them to get to us!"

Tyrone had not been thinking of that. As fast as they can, they turn the red fishing boat upside down again over the money. Carmen gets a stick and tries to make the beach look like it did before they came.

"All through?" asks Tyrone.

"I think so," Carmen answers. "I just don't want them to know we have been here."

"That's all the time we have to work on it," says Tyrone. "We really need to get back."

They run to the *Venus Light,* and — with another **1–2–3, go**! — they are off. Tyrone gets the map out and tells Carmen how to get back to Spider's Point. Some time after, she sees the lighthouse and knows they are just about home.

When they beach the boat, Carmen gets out as fast as she can and runs for Sunquest Drive. "I'll meet you back here when I get my dad," she calls out to Ty. "Just stay here!"

"I'll get Gran," calls Tyrone, "and tell her about everything while we wait for you!"

He looks after Carmen as she runs to the shelter. When he can no longer see her, he heads up the beach to the house and to Gran.

"Gran?" he calls out as he comes in the door.

There is no answer.

"Gran?" he calls again. Nothing. *She's not here!*

Tyrone runs back outside and looks up and down the beach. Is she reading somewhere? Fishing? Cooking? Sleeping? He looks every place he can think of, but Gran is not here. He looks again through the beach house.

Does anything look different? he thinks. No. Everything is just as Gran would have had it.

Ty walks into the kitchen to get a glass of water, then sits down to wait for Carmen and Tom Champion. *What's taking so long?* he thinks. *She should be back by now!*

When enough time has passed, Tyrone heads to the front door and down Sunquest to the shelter. *I'll just meet them there,* he thinks.

But when he gets to the animal shelter, Ty knows something has gone wrong. The door is open, and the animals are going out of their minds.

Everything in the shelter has been smashed! Tom Champion's PC is on the floor, and his charts are all over the place!

"Carmen!" Ty screams. "Where are you?" He calls and calls, but not a sound comes back.

12. On His Own

All Tyrone can think about as he races back to the beach house is that the Champions have been taken. *It was a trap!* he thinks. At the house, Tyrone looks in again to see if Gran is there. Again, nothing. *Maybe they have her too!* He runs into the bedroom and kitchen to get whatever he thinks he may need, then starts for the door. Thinking again, he runs back to the kitchen and writes Gran a fast letter to tell her what's going on. *Just in case,* he thinks.

Then he races off to the *Venus Light* and goes out into the water. *I can do this!* he says over and over to himself. *I know I can!* He smashes into and around the waves and gets out into the open sea. When he is close to the lighthouse, he remembers to get his headings — NNE. *That's right!* he says to himself. Going by the map, Tyrone makes his way over the sea to try to find his friends and Grandma.

I hope they're all right! Tyrone thinks. *Maybe I should have gone to the cops first. No, there just was not enough time. On the other hand*—All the way there, over each wave, Tyrone's mind fights within him.

His body starts to feel like the waves are trying to attack him! **In** comes the water, **over** the boat, **into** his eyes, and **over** his head! Time after time, hit after hit, Tyrone thinks he is done for. *It didn't look this hard when Carmen was doing it!* But Ty sticks with it, and keeps the *Venus Light* on course.

It's not long before he sees the beach — far away, but what a pretty picture! He puts the map away, using the beach as his lifeline. The closer he gets, however, the more he thinks something looks different.

"The red wooden fishing boat!" Ty calls out. "It's gone!" Scared as can be and still fighting with the sea, Ty wills his boat faster through the water. In the end, the water helps him out by throwing the boat up onto the beach with a big wave, and Ty gets out as fast as he can. He pulls it all the way up before he falls down himself. *Enough!* he thinks. *I can't move.*

But thinking of Tom Champion and Carmen gets him up and going. He looks everywhere for the red boat. *I know it was right here on the dark part of the beach!* he thinks. Then he studies things a little closer. He sees where people have walked away from this part of the beach!

Scared for his friends and his Gran, Ty makes his way along the dark beach.

13. Help? or Help!

It feels to Tyrone like he has to walk forever, not knowing that he is even going the right way! The beach gives way to plants and other green things, then woods. Every now and then, Ty stops to see if he hears anything. He doesn't want to call out if the bad guys are anywhere around.

Feeling lost and upside down, it comes to Ty that he has nothing to lose. He has to find Gran, Carmen, and Tom. "Carmen!" he calls out, a little low at first. Then, "Gran?" He stops in the woods, hoping to hear sounds. *Did I hear something that time?* he thinks. "**Carmen!**" he calls out. "**Tom Champion!**" he screams. *There! Just then! I did hear something!*

Ty runs to the sound. Over there — on the right! At last he sees the Champions!

"I'm here!" he screams, running up to help them. He sees Carmen, sitting up. It looks like her dad is sleeping on some leaves. Ty looks around, but he does not see Gran. He goes to Carmen first, because it looks as if something was put over her mouth to keep her from screaming for help. "Here," says Tyrone, "let me get this off." As soon as he pulls it off, he asks, "Are you OK, Carmen? Did they harm you?"

"N-N-No," she tells him, "I think I'm OK, but my dad—I think they gave him a drug!" They run to Carmen's dad. "He has not moved at all, Ty!" she cries. "Dad!" she screams. "Dad, get up!"

Tyrone looks Tom Champion over, then tries to make Carmen feel better. "I think he's OK, Carmen. He's going to be all right."

"You think?" she says. Tyrone puts his hand on her face and smiles.

"Really," he says. "I think they just gave him a drug to put him to sleep for a while."

Carmen tries to smile, but she has been through too much.

"We need to get back," says Tyrone. "The *Venus Light* is down at the beach. We will take her back to Gran's house and call the cops right away. Can you help me with your dad?"

Together, one on each side, they help Tom Champion get up. They try to help him walk back, little by little, to the beach from the woods. It takes a long while, and from time to time Carmen and Tyrone have to stop and sit. At last, Ty hears the waves and knows they are close.

Nothing has ever looked as good to Carmen as the *Venus Light*. "She was pretty anyway," Carmen says, laughing a little, "but she's like a pretty painting to me now! I feel hope for the first time in a while."

They take Carmen's dad, who is coming out of his sleep, to the boat and help him in. Then Tyrone and Carmen look at each other over the boat.

"1–2–3?" asks Carmen.

Tyrone just laughs as they put their hands on the sides of the boat to start the run into the water.

"Going anywhere?" The 2 turn as they hear a mean laugh. Tyrone and Carmen see 2 men walk over to them. Ty closes his eyes. It's the guys who were in a fight on Sunquest Drive — Red Overlook and the other man. *I knew it*, thinks Ty, *I just knew it was them.* Ty and Carmen can't run. Tom Champion is better, but he is still not well enough to run.

14. Where Are the Good Guys?

"All right, you three," says Red. "Hands on your heads and walk this way."

Tyrone and Carmen do not know what to do. There is no telling how far these men will go when so much money is on the line. "Just do as they say," Tyrone tells Carmen. "I'll think of something."

"You will do **nothing**, kid," says the one called Red. "You will just do what I say or somebody gets it."

Red pulls at Tom Champion, and Tyrone and Carmen walk next to them into the darkest part of the beach. Ty sees that the men have placed the box of money in front of them.

"I knew we would get all three of them," says Red to the other man, "if we waited long enough. Right, Don?"

"Right, boss," says Don.

"Take this and put it on them," Red says to Don, "and make it so they can't get away."

"You got it, boss," says Don.

"You need to keep out of things that aren't yours," says Red. "Like maps and money and red fishing boats."

"Just let us go!" cries Carmen. "We don't want the money!"

"Sorry—we can't leave you around here," says Red. "Not when you know so much." He looks at Tom Champion. "We are going to give you a look at sharks that you would never see on the *Sea Dog*, my man!" This makes Red laugh.

Knowing now that their lives are on the line, Carmen lets out a scream that puts a stop to their laughing. "Good try, kid," says Red, now mad, "but you can scream your head off. There is no one around to hear you." Then he turns to Don. "Let's just get them out on the boat and throw them over the side when we get out to sea."

Don and Red order Carmen and Ty back to the boat. "Take Champion with you!" they order. "Now, move it!"

The 2 kids get up and try to help Carmen's dad. It's not as hard now that he is not so asleep. They walk as they did coming back to the beach, Ty and Carmen on each side of her dad.

"What are we going to do?" asks Carmen.

"I'm thinking!" says Tyrone.

"Stop talking!" screams Red. "Just get in the boat!"

"We are going to have to run!" says Ty. "It's all we have got! 1–2–3–"

"Hold it right there!" says someone new. "Don't even move."

It's the cops!

Carmen falls to the beach, scared and happy at the same time. Tom Champion puts his head down on the side of the boat and cries, knowing that they are all safe. Ty runs around the boat to Carmen and takes her by the hand. "Everything's going to be all right now," he tells her, "because the good guys are here at last!"

"Hold it right there!"

15. Safe at Last

"How did you know where to find us?" asks Tyrone.

"Well," says the first cop, "we had a little help with that."

"What kind of help?" Ty wants to know.

With that, Grandma Inez walks up from behind, crying and going to Tyrone.

"I'm so happy you are safe, Ty," she says, her eyes full.

"No," smiles Ty. "I'm happy **you're** safe. I was thinking those men had taken, you too, Gran!"

"No, no, I had just gone into Spider's Point for some things," says Gran. "When I got back to the house, I looked in the kitchen and saw your letter. I read it and ran right back to the Point to get some help."

Ty turns to the cops. "But I don't get it," he says. "How did you know where to come without the map?"

"I can help with that," says one of the cops. "You see, we have had our eyes on Red Overlook and his friend for more than 2 weeks. We knew they had taken the money from the bank," he goes on, "but we had no idea where they had put it. So, we made it our job to know what he's been up to, hoping he would take us to the money."

"As soon as Mrs. Card came in to show us your letter," another cop tells them, "we knew that we had to make our move today — and fast! I called a team of men to take down Red and Don, but we had to get them in the right places to make it safe for everyone. You see," laughs the cop, "when you came along, Ty, we had to find the money **and** keep three people safe. That's a job!"

The cop turns to Carmen. "I'm really, really sorry you had to go through all of this," he says. "If there were any other way, we would have done it. I'm just happy you're all OK."

"You did a good job," says Tom Champion. "I have never been as happy to see cops in my life as I was to see you three today."

"Dad," says Carmen, "I do think you need to see someone. You don't look like yourself, and who knows what those men put in the drug they gave you!"

"You're right," says the cop, "and help is on the way for him. In fact, let's get in the boat, and we will take you kids home as well."

"What about my boat?" asks Tyrone.

"Sorry," says the cop. "We don't have what we need here to get your boat home right now. We will have to come back for it tonight."

Ty looks back to the *Venus Light*. "No, you guys go ahead," he says. "I think I'll take the *Venus Light* home myself."

"That's OK," says the first cop, "but we will need you to come in tonight so we can write up a summary and clean up some of these details."

"No problem," Tyrone tells them. "I'll be there."

"Want a little help with the *Venus Light*?" asks Carmen. "It's been said that I'm pretty good with boats."

"By who?" laughs Tyrone.

"By me, of course!" says Carmen.

"Now, Carmen," says her dad, "I don't think—"

"We will be OK, Dad," says Carmen. "Red Overlook and his friend Don are in good hands now." She smiles at the cops. "Right?"

"The best," laughs one of the cops. "They won't be going anywhere for a long, long time."

"Well," says Dad, "as long as those madmen are out of the picture, I guess it would be all right. But be careful, kids—no kidding."

"We will be careful," says Tyrone. "And you, Gran—do you mind?"

"I guess not," says Gran. "Take care and go on, but you need to be back at the beach house by 6:30."

"Why is that?" asks Ty.

"Because someone is coming to see you," Gran tells him.

"Can I ask who?" says Tyrone.

"No, you can't," Gran says with a smile.

16. A Home on Spider's Point

"I'm really sorry this had to go on while you're on Spider's Point, Ty," says Carmen.

Tyrone closes his eyes and turns his face up to the sun, drinking in the pretty day. "It could have been anywhere," he says at last.

"Does this mean that you will go home to your mom and dad right away?" she asks, looking out over the sea from the *Venus Light.*

"No," says Tyrone. "I think Gran needs me."

"I know she **wants** you here," says Carmen. "She was **so** happy that you were going to come."

"You know, it's interesting how life turns out different than you think," Tyrone says. "At first, I didn't want to come here at all. I was thinking my time on Spider's Point was going to be **so** long and **so** bad."

"I didn't know that!" kids Carmen, laughing. "When I first saw you, you were so happy, like you were on — Venus!"

Tyrone laughs too. "I guess I was, in a way — I was going to the *Venus Light*. I can't believe there was ever a time that I didn't want to be here."

"Well, while no one is around," says Carmen, "I just wanted to tell you that I'm happy you came. For someone who started out being kind of a monster, you ended up being a pretty good guy."

"I try," says Tyrone with a smile. "But now we had better get back to the beach house. Gran says someone is coming to see me."

Together, they put the *Venus Light* up on the beach, then pull the boat up by the house.

"Now, **that** takes me back a long, long time," says someone coming out of Gran's house.

"Dad!" screams Tyrone. "What are you doing here?"

"What about me?" says someone behind his dad.

"Mom! I can't believe it!"

Hand in hand, Tyrone's mom and dad walk down from the house to Carmen and Ty, who are waiting by the *Venus Light*.

"Does this—are you saying—what I mean is"—Ty tries to get out—"is everything OK now?"

"Everything is OK, Tyrone," says Mom. "We have talked it all out now, and we are ready to move on together." Dad and Mom smile at each other, then at the kids.

"It's a long story, but I ran away from Spider's Point many years ago," says Dad. "And now, for the life of me, I can't remember why! All I know is, it feels so **good** to be back."

Carmen looks down, feeling sad as she thinks of Tyrone going back with his family. "How long can you be here before you have to go?" she asks at last.

"Go?" says Gran, walking out to be with everyone else. "Who said anything about going?"

Dad looks at Tyrone. "Grandma has asked us to stay and help her out here."

"No kidding?" asks Ty.

"No kidding!" laugh Mom and Dad. "What do you think?"

Tyrone looks at Dad. "I think that we need to go out on the *Venus Light*, that's what I think!" says Ty. "You have a few things to show me, you racer-dad, you!"

"You're on!" says Dad.

"By the way," asks Ty as they walk to the boat, "has Gran said anything about our day?"

"Why, no," Dad answers. "Is there anything to tell?"

Tyrone looks back at Carmen, Mom, and Grandma Inez on the beach, then at his dad.

"Let's just say you're not the only one with a long story, Dad," says Ty with a smile. "But nothing that can't wait." Ty gives a big laugh. "Nothing at all that can't wait."